Play

When rhinos play together, their actions can be very physical. Since rhinos cannot see very well, play involves close contact. It can include close chases, friendly pushes, or splashing in the water.

Take a Stand
·Debate·
·Research·

Does tourism help to save rhinos?

Many tourists take African safaris to get a chance to view rhinos and other animals in their natural habitat. White rhinos are somewhat easier to find because they graze on open grasslands. Black rhinos are more difficult to see in their wooded habitat. Tour guides keep in radio contact with one another and report sightings so that more of the tourists have the opportunity to see rhinos.

FOR

1. People who get a chance to see these animals in nature start to care more about their survival. These people will want to protect rhinos from extinction.
2. Safari and game-watching tours provide income for local people. This helps remove the temptation to break the law and try to make money by hunting rhinos for their horns.

AGAINST

1. Guides want to please their clients, and they may bring tourists too close to the animals just for a better photo, upsetting the rhinos.
2. Using large vehicles may damage the land, including the plants rhinos need for food.

Horned
Wonders

In general, the larger the animal, the longer it carries a baby before birth. For rabbits, the **gestation period** is about one month. Lions carry their young for a little more than three months. For rhinos, the gestation period is about 15 to 16 months.

White rhinos give birth to a new calf about every two to three years.

Mating and Birth

Rhinos can mate and give birth at any time of the year. In some areas, however, mating is more common at certain times. In Kenya, for example, black rhino mating is most common from September to November. In South Africa, it is more common from April to July.

When a male first approaches a female rhino to mate, she will often be aggressive, even to the point of attacking. A male approaches with caution, stopping and snorting. The female may chase him off with short charges until she is ready to mate. The male runs away but returns again and again until the female is ready to accept him.

During the mating period, an adult male and female form a temporary group. If the female still has a calf with her, the three of them may form a group for a while, or the male may chase the young rhino away from its mother. When females are pregnant, they may either get very aggressive toward males or just avoid them. Rhinos will go into hiding when they are about to give birth.

A newborn white rhino will be able to follow its mother just a couple of days after its birth.

Calves

Both black and white rhinos give birth to one calf at a time. After a rhino calf is born, the mother often licks it clean. It can stand up when it is about an hour old, and it takes its first steps soon after.

A black rhino calf usually follows its mother wherever she goes. This is different from the behavior of a white rhino calf, which walks a few steps ahead of its mother. The difference may be due to the two species' habitats. Black rhino mothers clear a path through the bushes as they walk, making it easier for their young to follow them. White rhinos usually walk through grass, so this path clearing is not important. Sometimes, a black rhino mother will leave her calf in bushes or another hiding place while she goes to drink or **browse**.

White rhinos can weigh up to 145 pounds (65 kg) when they are born. Black rhino calves weigh between 60 and 100 pounds (27 and 45 kg) at birth. A calf usually begins nursing within a few hours of birth. Rhino calves will drink milk while their mother is standing up or lying down. When they are about a week and a half old, calves may also start nibbling at plants. By the time calves are about three weeks old, they have already learned to wallow, or roll around, in the mud.

During its first four months of life, a calf gains about 3 pounds (1.4 kg) a day.

Horned
Wonders

While few predators are brave enough to take on an adult white or black rhino, calves are often attacked. As a result, calves learn to stay close to their mothers at all times.

A young calf can drink up to 6 gallons (23 liters) of its mother's milk each day.

Horned
Wonders

White rhinos, if undisturbed, live 40 years to 50 years in nature. Black rhinos live 30 to 40 years in their natural habitat.

Indian and white rhino calves are the tallest at birth, with an average height of 2 feet (0.6 m).

Development

Although it begins to eat more and more plants as it grows, a rhino calf will continue to nurse from its mother. Nursing may go on until the calf is 2 years old. A young rhino will stay with its mother even after it is **weaned**.

When a calf is 4 months old, its nose horn is about 1.5 inches (4 cm) long. After 5 months, the second horn begins to show. By the time the calf is 6 months old, the second horn is about 0.5 inch (1.3 cm) long, and by 8 months, it is about 1 inch (2.5 cm) long.

Once the calf is 2 to 5 years old, it is often forced to leave its mother. This often happens when the mother mates or when a new calf is born. The calf may then join other calves or a single female until it is full-grown and goes off to live on its own. Even after the birth of the next calf, a young rhino may still return to join its mother, especially if the youngster is female.

By 3 years of age, a calf is almost as big as its mother, but it will not be full-grown until it is about 7 years old. Female black rhinos do not usually have calves until they are more than 4 years old. Female white rhinos will begin having calves at 6 to 7 years old.

Young white rhino calves often play by themselves but never too far from their mothers.

Habitat

White rhinos like the flat open land of a **savanna**, where they can find grass, water, and some bushes and trees. They use the bushy areas during the day, when they rest in the shade. Nearby grasslands are used for grazing in the morning and evening. Water sources are important for drinking and wallowing. In times of **drought**, white rhinos will follow a narrow path from their home range to another nearby water source every few days.

Black rhinos can live in many different types of African habitats, but they are most commonly found on the edges of wooded areas or in other areas where there is some cover. Most black rhinos prefer areas that are not too dry and not too hot. This may be because these habitats have more of the food they like to eat. Black rhinos are sometimes found on the slopes of mountains, as high up as 9,000 feet (2,750 m).

Organizing the Savanna

Earth is home to millions of different **organisms**, all of which have specific survival needs. These organisms rely on their environment, or the place where they live, for their survival. All plants and animals have relationships with their environment. They interact with the environment itself, as well as the other plants and animals within the environment. These interactions create **ecosystems**.

Ecosystems can be broken down into levels of organization. These levels range from a single plant or animal to many species of plants and animals living together in an area.

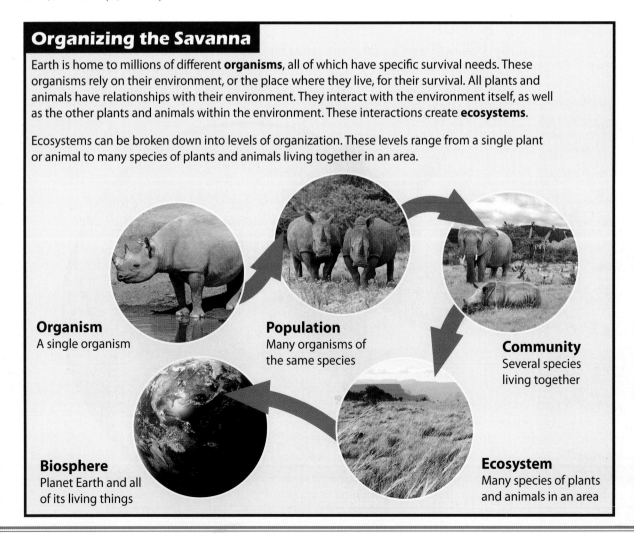

Organism
A single organism

Population
Many organisms of the same species

Community
Several species living together

Biosphere
Planet Earth and all of its living things

Ecosystem
Many species of plants and animals in an area

Horned
Wonders

Indian rhinos mostly live in grasslands but can also be found in swamps and forests. Javan and Sumatran rhinos prefer lowland tropical forests. Sumatran rhinos may move to hilly areas at certain times if lowland areas flood.

Adult white rhinos can spend their entire lives in the same area unless water holes dry up.

Horned
Wonders

Male Sumatran rhinos have territories as large as 19 square miles (49 square kilometers). Females' territories are much smaller, ranging from 4 to 6 square miles (10 to 15 sq. km).

White rhinos have larger heads than the other rhino species. Partly as a result of the weight of their heads, white rhinos have developed strong muscles in their necks.

Range

Rhinos usually stay within their own home range. Except for dominant males, their range can overlap with those of other rhinos. Rhinos must live near water, and because water can be scarce in their habitats, several rhinos will often use the same water hole. Rhinos know which other rhinos are their neighbors. They will tolerate each other. Male rhinos tend to fight only with new males coming into their area.

For white and black rhinos, the size of a home range depends upon the characteristics of the habitat. In areas where there is more to eat and plenty of water, a home range may be only 1 square mile (2.6 sq. km). Where there is less to eat, it may be as big as 50 square miles (130 sq. km). Within their home range, rhinos have favorite spots that they use more often than others. During the day, a rhino tends to be less active and uses only a small area within its home range. At night, it is usually more active, using more of its range.

The Northern white rhino once lived throughout north-central Africa south of the Sahara Desert. It is now the most rare of all of the African rhinos. It may soon be considered extinct in nature. There may be so few of the animals left in the world that there is not enough **genetic** variation for the subspecies to survive. It has been several years since any Northern white rhinos were seen outside of protected areas, and only a few captive Northern white rhinos remain in a reserve in Kenya. The Southern white rhino, however, is the most numerous of all the world's rhinos. Once found in most of Africa south of the Sahara, this subspecies now lives mostly in South Africa.

Black rhinos once roamed most of Africa south of the Sahara. Today, the three remaining subspecies are found only in small pockets of land. These areas are in the southern and eastern parts of the continent.

From an Expert

"The rhinoceros, throughout its historical range, has been hunted for its horn and is now on the brink of extinction as a result." - Mark Atkinson

Mark Atkinson is a wildlife veterinarian from Zimbabwe. He has worked on rhino conservation projects for Zimbabwe's Department of National Parks and Wildlife Management.

Migration

Rhinos are creatures of habit. They like to use the same trails through the forest or across grassland. Most rhinos browse or graze starting early in the morning. At midday, the rhinos rest in the shade. Later in the afternoon, the rhinos cool off with a mud bath and then start to feed again. This daily routine rarely changes.

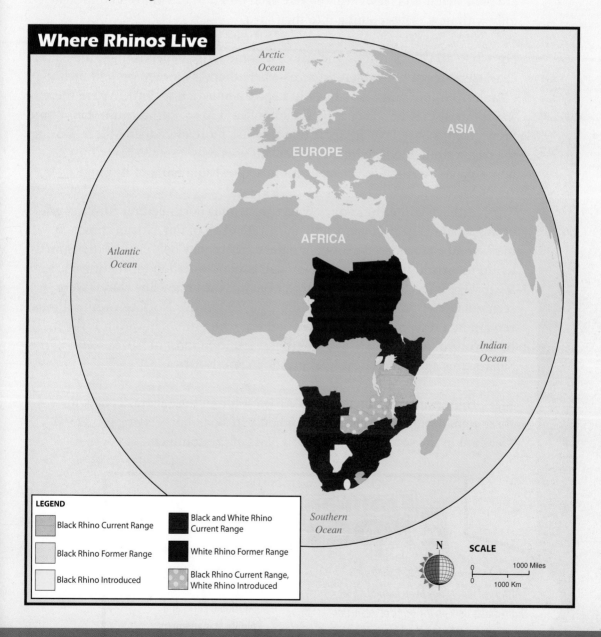

Where Rhinos Live

LEGEND

- Black Rhino Current Range
- Black Rhino Former Range
- Black Rhino Introduced
- Black and White Rhino Current Range
- White Rhino Former Range
- Black Rhino Current Range, White Rhino Introduced

SCALE

0   1000 Miles

0   1000 Km

Rhinos may use different parts of their home range during different seasons. During the dry season, rhinos must stay close to a water hole, usually within 3 miles (5 km). They also tend to eat more plants that store water in their roots and stems. A rhino will sometimes walk miles to find a new water source in times of drought. However, a rhino will not migrate permanently out of its home range, even if its water disappears. In the rainy season, rhinos are able to travel farther away from a reliable water source.

Habitat loss has forced the Javan rhino to live in only small parts of its former territory. Remaining populations are found in the countries of Indonesia and Vietnam.

Take a Stand
Debate · *Research*

Should clearing land for farming be limited in order to protect rhino habitats?

People in Africa are clearing more and more land for farming. Some of this land is in areas where rhinos have been living. The rhinos are left with less land in which to find food, water, and other things they need to survive.

FOR

1. Besides hunting, loss of their natural habitats is one the biggest threats to rhino populations. These habitats need to be preserved to keep rhinos from becoming extinct.
2. Farms require water for crops. During dry seasons, rhinos travel over larger areas to find water. If people are living and farming near water holes, this limits their use by animals such as rhinos.

AGAINST

1. Raising crops for food is a necessary part of life. As the population grows, so does the need for more farmland. The needs of people must come first.
2. The majority of African rhinos are now found in protected parks and game reserves where clearing land for farming is already not allowed.

Diet

All rhinos are **herbivores**. Like many animals that eat plants, rhinos digest their food slowly. Rhinos are big animals that need to eat a great deal of food each day, so they tend to eat alone. This way, they are not competing with other rhinos for food. Black and white rhinos eat different types of plants. White rhinos eat mostly short grasses. Black rhinos eat parts of trees and shrubs instead of short grass. What they eat changes depending on the season and on what is available in each rhino's area.

Black rhinos browse on woody shrubs, small trees, and plants with broad leaves. They will also eat fruit. They sometimes take in grass when they are eating other plants, but grass is not an important part of their diet. If they are in open grasslands, they will occasionally feed on clumps of long grass. Black rhinos usually eat more than 50 pounds (23 kg) of vegetation each day. To get all this food, they eat many different species of plants. In some regions, black rhinos are known to eat more than 200 different species of plants. They can even eat plants that have special, bad-tasting chemicals in them that protect the plants from being eaten by most other animals.

A black rhino uses its upper lip to pull bits off trees and other plants. It even uses its lip to pull fruit out of trees. By stepping on small trees, a black rhino brings the higher branches into reach. It also uses its horns to pull branches down. In more open areas, a black rhino may eat small, newly growing trees. It pulls these saplings right out of the ground with its mouth.

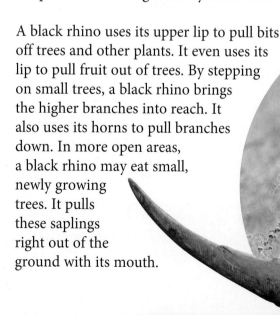

A white rhino spends more than 12 hours a day grazing.

Horned
Wonders

Indian rhinos eat mainly grasses but also some fruit, leaves, and tree branches.

In the past, Indian rhinos were common in northwestern India and Pakistan. Today, they are found in only a few small areas of northern India and Nepal.

The Food Cycle

A food cycle shows how energy in the form of food is passed from one living thing to another. As rhinos browse or graze and move through forests and grasslands, they affect the lives of other living things. In the diagram below, the arrows show the flow of energy from one living thing to the next through a **food web**.

Producers
Grasses, shrubs, and trees use energy from sunlight and nutrients in the soil to grow and produce food energy.

Secondary Consumers
Rhinos, particularly the young, are sometimes hunted and eaten by lions and hyenas. After lions and hyenas have had their fill, scavengers such as vultures come in to pick the carcass clean.

Primary Consumers
White rhinos get the energy they need to live and grow by eating grasses. Black rhinos get food energy by browsing on leafy plants and tree branches.

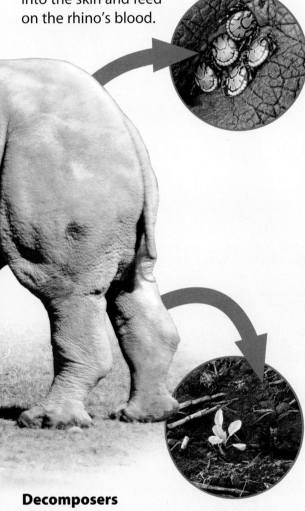

Parasites

The thick, wrinkled skin of the rhinoceros is home to many different parasites, including more than 20 different species of ticks. Ticks burrow into the skin and feed on the rhino's blood.

Decomposers

When a rhinoceros dies, the parts of its body that are left by scavengers are broken down by decomposers. This adds nutrients to the soil, which helps grassland and forest plants to grow.

Take a Stand

·Debate·
·Research·

Are protected parks and game reserves with heavy security the answer to saving rhino populations?

As part of conservation efforts in many parts of Africa, some rhinos are being moved into well-protected parks and game reserves that are patrolled by armed guards and anti-poaching teams.

FOR

1. In 1900, the Southern white rhino was one of the most **endangered** rhino subspecies. Once this rhino became protected in parks and reserves, its numbers came back. There were more than 20,000 in 2012.
2. As a result of human activities in rhino habitats, experience shows that very few rhinos survive outside of national parks and reserves.

AGAINST

1. Protected, managed game reserves do not totally eliminate poaching. Many rhinos are poached after wandering off a reserve looking for food or water during a drought. Laws do not protect them when they step outside the reserve.
2. Civil war and political unrest in many areas of Africa make enforcing conservation laws extremely difficult. Poachers often are not single individuals, but well-armed gangs. They have better weapons than the guards and can take rhinos even in parks and reserves.

When male white rhinos fight, their very long
horns can cause serious damage to an opponent.

Animals on the Brink

Competition

Rhinos are not usually aggressive toward each other. When two rhinos meet, they may bump with their heads. Sometimes, they bump with the sides of their horns. After this, they usually walk away from each other.

White rhinos and black rhinos are sometimes found in the same areas. When this happens, there is little competition between the two species. Black rhinos are browsers, so they do not need to compete for food with the grazing white rhinos.

When two males meet, they may snort, paw the ground, sweep their heads back and forth, and push their horns in the air. Then, they might make short charges that stop before they reach each other. After a tense standoff, one of them often walks away.

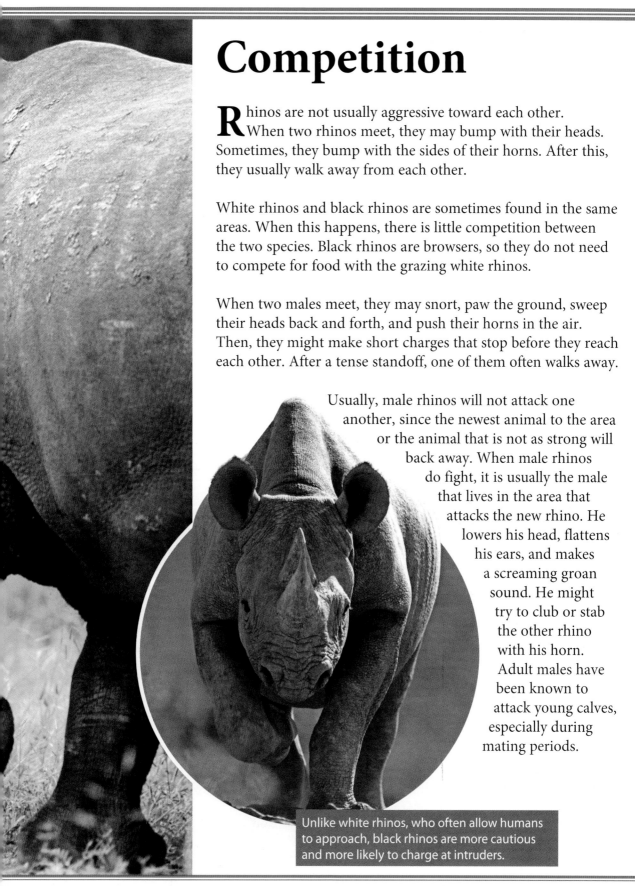

Usually, male rhinos will not attack one another, since the newest animal to the area or the animal that is not as strong will back away. When male rhinos do fight, it is usually the male that lives in the area that attacks the new rhino. He lowers his head, flattens his ears, and makes a screaming groan sound. He might try to club or stab the other rhino with his horn. Adult males have been known to attack young calves, especially during mating periods.

Unlike white rhinos, who often allow humans to approach, black rhinos are more cautious and more likely to charge at intruders.

Rhinos with Other Animals

Adult rhinos have few enemies. They are rarely attacked, but young rhinos are sometimes taken by predators. Mother rhinos protect their young and will even threaten or charge a lion. Lions have been known to attack adult rhinos, but this is not very common. There have been reports of adult rhinos being fatally injured by crocodiles, but this is also rare. In general, humans are the only real threat to rhinos.

Both black and white rhinos are often seen with small gray-brown birds sitting on their backs. These birds, called oxpeckers, help the rhinos by eating the parasites on their skin. The rhinos have so many parasites that they provide a continuous source of food for the birds. Oxpeckers also warn the rhinos of approaching danger. The birds can see much better and farther than the rhinos, and they make loud calls when they are alarmed. The cattle egret eats insects that fly around the rhino. It is common to see this white bird sitting on a rhino's back.

To make up for their poor eyesight, rhinos have also learned to respond to the alarm reactions of other ungulates. Sometimes, rhinos feed near buffalo. This feeding habit may help protect them from unseen dangers. The buffalo has much better vision than the rhino and will see a predator long before the rhino does.

Humans are the rhino's greatest threat. For centuries, people have hunted rhinos for food. In recent decades, large numbers of rhinos have been taken for their horns. As a result, rhinos have learned to fear humans.

In addition to picking parasites off of a rhino's skin, oxpeckers also eat any ground insects found near the rhino's feet.

Horned
Wonders

Though Indian rhino calves may be taken by tigers, humans are still the main predator of Indian rhinos.

After elephants, rhinos are the second-largest land mammals. Both animals are not aggressive, but there have been cases when the two giants have clashed.

Folklore

For centuries, black and white rhinos have been part of the folklore of many different African cultures. Many folktales try to explain characteristics of the rhino that are different from other animals, such as its poor eyesight or wrinkled skin. Many stories focus on the rhino's size. Some stories do not show the rhino in a positive way. These stories sometimes claim that rhinos are bad-tempered and lazy. The tales often use rhinos as an example of what happens if people have these qualities.

In folktales, the rhino often loses out to the bigger elephant or to other animals that are considered to be smarter than the rhino. Rhinos are often shown as being slow or easily fooled. One folktale tells about a hare that tricks a hippopotamus and a rhinoceros into having a tug-of-war with each other without the two bigger animals knowing what is happening. In another tale, a rhino's bad manners result in its being tricked into wearing an itchy coat that it cannot take off.

One popular myth from Southeast Asia tells how rhinos put out fires. Many animals run away from a fire. In the myth, however, rhinos called *badak api*, meaning "fire rhinos," charge and stomp out fires. Though the myth shows how brave rhinos can be, there is likely no truth to it. Rhinos, like other animals, will flee from this type of danger.

Rhinos have been shown in art for thousands of years. Saint Mark's Basilica in Venice, Italy, has a rhino mosaic that is more than 1,000 years old.

Myth	**VS**	Fact
A rhino's skin is so thick that it is bulletproof.		Although rhino skin is thick, it is not bulletproof. This myth came from an early engraving of an Indian rhino. In the engraving, the rhino's skin looked like it was made of metal.
Rhino horn is a powerful medicine.		Rhino horn is used as a traditional medicine in parts of Asia and Africa. Scientists have reported, however, that rhino horn has no real healing properties.
Rhinos are slow and lazy.		Rhinos spend most of their time eating. They move slowly throughout their feeding areas. In the heat of the day, they rest. Their slow movements might make them appear lazy, but when they are nervous or angry, they can run almost as fast as a giraffe or a rabbit.

Ancient rock paintings found in the African country of Namibia show a variety of animals, including a rhinoceros.

Status

As the human population has grown in many parts of Africa, more and more land is being used for farming and for cities and towns. As a result, a great deal of the habitat of both white and black rhinos has been destroyed. Habitat loss is a serious problem for rhinos in Asia as well.

People also hunt white and black rhinos. In most cases, the animals are taken for their horns. Rhino horns have been valued for thousands of years. The ancient Greeks and Persians believed that rhino horns had magical powers. Some of these beliefs continue today in many Asian cultures. Scientists are trying to convince people that these myths are not true.

Hunting rhinos is now illegal or very limited in many African countries. Still, rhino horn sells for such high prices that poaching is a major problem. Poachers make so much money from selling rhino horns that they will risk their lives to hunt rhinos. So many animals have been taken by poachers and other hunters that rhinos around the world are struggling to survive.

According to the IUCN, three rhino species are critically endangered. They are the Sumatran, Javan, and black rhinos. In the late 1960s, it was estimated there were still about 70,000 black rhinos living in nature. Almost 95 percent of Africa's black rhinos were killed between 1970 and 1994, mostly for their horns. By 1991, there were fewer than 2,500 black rhinos left.

Rhinos of the World		
Species	**Status**	**Population in Nature**
White Rhino	Near Threatened	about 20,170
Black Rhino	Critically Endangered	about 4,880
Indian Rhino	Vulnerable	about 2,900
Sumatran Rhino	Critically Endangered	fewer than 250
Javan Rhino	Critically Endangered	fewer than 50

By 2012, the overall black rhino population had made a comeback. There were estimated to be more than 4,800 black rhinos. The West African black rhino subspecies, however, was declared extinct in 2011.

The white rhino is recovering from a record low number of about 100 animals in 1895. Today, there are more than 20,000 white rhinos living in Africa. The Northern white rhino subspecies, however, is on the verge of being declared extinct in nature. The last sightings in nature were four animals in Garamba National Park in 2006. For the Southern white rhino, poaching continues to be a huge problem and is actually on the rise in South Africa.

Guards in national parks and game reserves try to protect rhinos. In 2012, however, more than 600 rhinos were taken by poachers in South Africa.

Take a Stand
· Debate ·   · Research ·

Should rhinos have their horns removed to try to keep them safe from poachers?

Dehorning projects are sometimes carried out as part of larger efforts to save rhino populations. The rhinos are given a drug that puts them to sleep, and 70 to 80 percent of the horn is removed.

FOR

1. Rhinos with horns are poached even in areas with good law enforcement. Removing the horns makes an animal much less appealing for poachers. After a project in Zimbabwe in which rhino horns were removed, poaching decreased, and the black rhino population increased.
2. Rhinos sometimes lose their horns naturally and re-grow them over several years. Studies show that rhinos can still mate, raise young, and maintain their territories even after losing their horns.

AGAINST

1. By improving law enforcement in poaching areas, rhinos can be better protected without such a drastic procedure. Dehorned rhinos are sometimes still poached for any new horn growth.
2. The effects of dehorning have not yet been fully studied. Dehorning may change behaviors or the social structure of the population. Rhinos may be killed or extremely stressed by the capture, drugging, and dehorning operation.

In China and other parts of Asia, police try to stop illegal shipments of rhino horns from entering the country.

Animals on the Brink

Saving the Rhinoceros

Rhino horn has two main markets. It is sold in parts of Asia, such as China, Taiwan, and South Korea, for use in traditional medicines. It is also sold in Middle Eastern countries for use as handles in ceremonial knives.

Rhino horns can earn poachers large sums of money. Many poachers see the reward of illegally hunting rhinos as being much greater than the risk of getting caught. This is especially true in countries where there is extreme poverty with few opportunities for other types of work. In some parts of Africa, rebel groups fighting against their country's government use the money they make from poaching rhino horns to buy weapons and other supplies they need to fight their wars.

Conservation groups from all over the world are trying to protect the last remaining rhinos. Yemen, a country where many people once used rhino horns for their daggers, signed an agreement to no longer import rhino horns. Some dehorning programs have been successful in reducing poaching. Other conservation projects involve moving rhinos to well-protected reserves that can be better patrolled by well-trained and well-armed guards. Efforts to save the remaining rhinos also include undercover investigations to catch people who continue to buy rhino products from poachers. In addition, some conservation projects involve protecting the rhino's remaining natural habitats.

One of the most effective ways to protect rhinos is through education. Education programs try to convince people not to buy medicines, daggers, and other products that are made from rhino horn. Poachers and others who share the rhino's environment can learn that rhinos are worth more alive than dead, if they are allowed to share the benefits. These benefits include jobs related to nature tourism, national park management, and wildlife conservation.

From an Expert

Esmond Bradley Martin was vice-chairman of the African Rhino Specialist Group of the IUCN. He has investigated the trade in rhino parts throughout Asia and Africa.

"Because of the present demand for rhino horn and hide—and the high prices being paid for them—I fear that present conservation methods are not adequate to ensure a future for rhinos outside zoos or a few isolated reserves." - Esmond Bradley Martin

Back from the Brink

onservation efforts are helping to save the world's rhinos. The number of Southern white rhinos, for example, has grown in recent years, and new efforts are being made to stop poaching of this subspecies. Rhinos in many parts of Africa are being moved away from unsafe areas, where poachers are operating, to more secure locations. Most of these animals are brought to heavily protected parks and game reserves.

The African Rhino Specialist Group, which is part of the IUCN, provides advice and assists governments and organizations on the conservation of African rhinos. The group has developed a detailed plan for saving and increasing the numbers of white and black rhinos. The IUCN group also helps raise awareness of rhino conservation by educating the public.

You can help by learning more about the issues and supporting conservation groups working to protect rhinos. The International Rhino Foundation (IRF) is one of several groups working around the world to save rhinos from extinction. The IRF suggests that people interested in protecting rhinos could host fundraising events to raise awareness and money for rhino conservation. For more information, contact the IRF:

International Rhino Foundation
201 Main Street, Suite 2600
Fort Worth, TX 76102

After tens of thousands of black rhinos were killed in the late 20th century, some subspecies are slowly making a comeback.

Activity

Debating helps people think about ideas thoughtfully and carefully. When people debate, two sides take a different viewpoint on a subject. Each side takes turns presenting arguments to support its view.

Use the Take a Stand sections found throughout this book as a starting point for debate topics. Organize your friends or classmates into two teams. One team will argue in favor of the topic, and the other will argue against. Each team should research the issue thoroughly using reliable sources of information, including books, scientific journals, and trustworthy websites. Take notes of important facts that support your side of the debate. Prepare your argument using these facts to support your opinion.

During the debate, the members of each team are given a set amount of time to make their arguments. The team arguing the For side goes first. They have five minutes to present their case. All members of the team should participate equally. Then, the team arguing the Against side presents its arguments. Each team should take notes of the main points the other team argues.

After both teams have made their arguments, they get three minutes to prepare their rebuttals. Teams review their notes from the previous round. The teams focus on trying to disprove each of the main points made by the other team using solid facts. Each team gets three minutes to make its rebuttal. The team arguing the Against side goes first. Students and teachers watching the debate serve as judges. They should try to judge the debate fairly using a standard score sheet, such as the example below.

Criteria	Rate: 1-10	Sample Comments
1. Were the arguments well organized?	8	logical arguments, easy to follow
2. Did team members participate equally?	9	divided time evenly between members
3. Did team members speak loudly and clearly?	3	some members were difficult to hear
4. Were rebuttals specific to the other team's arguments?	6	rebuttals were specific, more facts needed
5. Was respect shown for the other team?	10	all members showed respect to the other team

Quiz

1. How many species of rhinos are found in the world today?

2. Do all rhinos have two horns?

3. What is a rhinoceros signaling when its ears are flat?

4. True or false? The easiest way to tell a white rhino from a black rhino is by its color.

5. Why do rhinos often have oxpeckers perched on their backs?

6. Which African rhino species, the black rhino or the white rhino, is the biggest?

7. Is scent an important part of communication for African rhinos?

8. Which rhino species currently has the highest population?

9. What are two reasons that rhinos are hunted for their horns?

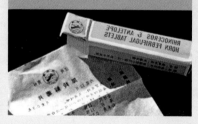

10. Besides poaching, what is another reason some rhino populations are shrinking?

Answers:
1. five (black, white, Javan, Sumatran, and Indian) 2. No. The Indian and Javan rhinos have only one horn. 3. Flat ears mean the rhino is angry. 4. False. Both types of rhinos are gray in color. 5. Oxpeckers eat parasites off the rhinos' skin. 6. White rhinos are the bigger of the two species. 7. Yes. Scent marking is one form of rhino communication. 8. the white rhino 9. Rhino horns are used in traditional medicines and as knife handles. 10. habitat loss

Key Words

browse: when an animal eats the shoots, twigs, and leaves off trees

drought: a long period of little or no rain

ecosystems: communities of living things and resources

endangered: at risk of no longer surviving in the world

extinction: no longer surviving in the world

family: one of eight major ranks used to classify animals

food web: connecting food chains that show how energy flows from one organism to another through diet

genetic: relating to characteristics passed down from one generation to the next through genes

gestation period: the length of time that a female is pregnant

graze: when an animal feeds on grass

habitats: places where animals live, grow, and raise their young

herbivores: animals that eat only plants

home range: the entire area in which an animal lives

mammals: warm-blooded animals that have hair or fur and nurse their young

nearsighted: capable of seeing nearby objects better than those found at a distance

nurse: when a young mammal drinks milk from its mother

order: one of eight major ranks used to classify animals, between class and family

organisms: forms of life

poachers: people who hunt an animal illegally

predators: animals that live by hunting other animals for food

prehensile: adapted for holding or grasping an object by wrapping around it

savanna: a tropical or subtropical grassy plain with only a few scattered trees

species: groups of individuals with common characteristics

ungulates: animals with hooves

weaned: when a young rhino does not drink milk from its mother anymore

Index

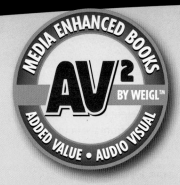

Log on to www.av2books.com

AV² by Weigl brings you media enhanced books that support active learning. Go to www.av2books.com, and enter the special code found on page 2 of this book. You will gain access to enriched and enhanced content that supplements and complements this book. Content includes video, audio, weblinks, quizzes, a slide show, and activities.

AV² Online Navigation

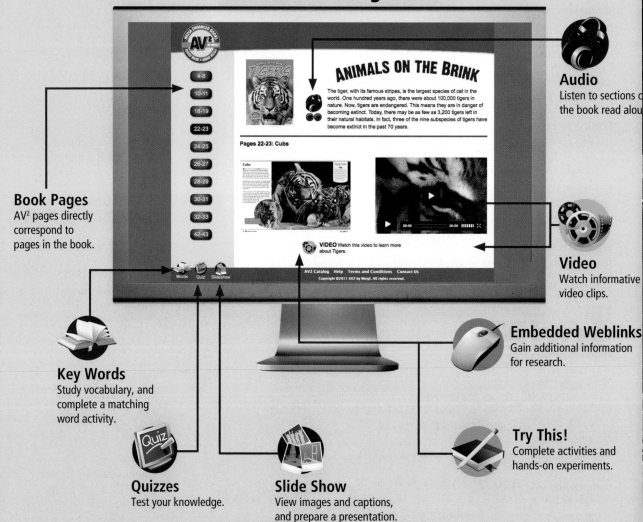

Book Pages
AV² pages directly correspond to pages in the book.

Audio
Listen to sections of the book read aloud

Video
Watch informative video clips.

Key Words
Study vocabulary, and complete a matching word activity.

Embedded Weblinks
Gain additional information for research.

Try This!
Complete activities and hands-on experiments.

Quizzes
Test your knowledge.

Slide Show
View images and captions, and prepare a presentation.

AV² was built to bridge the gap between print and digital. We encourage you to tell us what you like and what you want to see in the future.

Sign up to be an AV² Ambassador at www.av2books.com/ambassador.

Due to the dynamic nature of the Internet, some of the URLs and activities provided as part of AV² by Weigl may have changed or ceased to exist. AV² by Weigl accepts no responsibility for any such changes. All media enhanced books are regularly monitored to update addresses and sites in a timely manner. Contact AV² by Weigl at 1-866-649-3445 or av2books@weigl.com with any questions, comments, or feedback.